EAST GREENBUSH COMMUNITY LIBRARY

EAST GREENBUSH COMMUNITY LIBRARY

Priscilla Hauser's
BOOK
OF
Painting Patterns

Priscilla Hauser's
BOOK
OF
Painting Patterns

Priscilla Hauser

Sterling Publishing Co., Inc.
New York

Prolific Impressions Production Staff:
Editor in Chief: Mickey Baskett
Copy Editor: Phyllis Mueller
Graphics: Karen Turpin
Styling: Lenos Key
Photography: Jerry Mucklow
Administration: Jim Baskett

Every effort has been made to insure that the information presented is accurate. Since we have no control over physical conditions, individual skills, or chosen tools and products, the publisher disclaims any liability for injuries, losses, untoward results, or any other damages which may result from the use of the information in this book. Thoroughly read the instructions for all products used to complete the projects in this book, paying particular attention to all cautions and warnings shown for that product to ensure their proper and safe use.

No part of this book may be reproduced for commercial purposes in any form without permission by the copyright holder. The written instructions and design patterns in this book are intended for the personal use of the reader and may be reproduced for that purpose only.

Library of Congress Cataloging-in-Publication Data:
Hauser, Priscilla.
   Priscilla Hauser's book of painting patterns.
      p. cm.
   Includes index.
   ISBN-13: 978-1-4027-1476-4
   ISBN-10: 1-4027-1476-9
1. Painting--Technique. 2. Decoration and ornament. I. Title: book of painting patterns

TT385.H375 2006
745.7'23--dc22

2005031366

10 9 8 7 6 5 4 3 2 1

Published by Sterling Publishing Co., Inc.
387 Park Avenue South, New York, N.Y. 10016
©2006 by Prolific Impressions, Inc.
Produced by Prolific Impressions, Inc.
160 South Candler St., Decatur, GA 30030
Distributed in Canada by Sterling Publishing
c/o Canadian Manda Group, 165 Dufferin Street
Toronto, Ontario, Canada M6K 3H6
Distributed in the United Kingdom by GMC Distribution Services,
Castle Place, 166 High Street, Lewes, East Sussex, England BN7 1XU
Distributed in Australia by Capricorn Link (Australia) Pty. Ltd.
P.O. Box 704, Windsor, NSW 2756 Australia

Printed in China
All rights reserved

Sterling ISBN-13: 978-1-4027-1476-4
          ISBN-10: 1-4027-1476-9

For information about custom editions, special sales, premium and corporate purchases, please contact Sterling Special Sales Department at 800-805-5489 or specialsales@sterlingpub.com.

CONTENTS

USING THE PATTERNS

This book contains more than 100 patterns that can be used for painting designs on all kinds of surfaces. There are patterns for dozens of flowers, fruits, animals, and vegetables, plus a section for holiday decorating and a section that includes borders, leaves, landscapes, and folk art stroke designs.

I've included my techniques and tips for transferring patterns, selecting paints and mediums for a variety of surfaces, and choosing and caring for brushes. You'll also find information on the painting supplies I find indispensable, and my techniques for floating, shading and highlighting, blending, flyspecking, and finishing. To help you get a proper start, there's also a section preparing surfaces that includes wood, glass and ceramics, metal, and fabric.

I hope this book can help you discover how much fun it is to create your own painted treasures.

Transferring Patterns

Transferring a Design with Transfer Paper

It is fine to transfer designs to a surface with white or gray transfer paper; however, this is my least favorite way to transfer a design because transfer paper tends to smudge. Here's how to use transfer paper:

1. Trace the pattern neatly and carefully from the book on tracing paper, using a pencil or fine point marker.
2. Position tracing on surface. Secure with tape.
3. Slide the transfer paper under the tracing with the transfer side facing the surface.
4. Using a stylus, neatly trace over the pattern lines to transfer the lines to the surface.

Tracing a pattern onto transfer paper. It is not necessary to trace shading lines or curlicues.

Transferring with a Charcoal Pencil

1. Neatly trace the pattern of the design onto tracing paper. You may use a pencil or a pen.
2. Turn over the traced design. Firmly go over the traced lines on the back with a charcoal pencil. (Photo 1)
3. Position the design on the prepared surface, charcoal side down. Using a stylus, go over the lines. (Photo 2)

Don't press so hard that you make indentations in the surface. The pattern lines will be transferred to your surface.

Photo 1 – Charcoal Pencil Method

Photo 2 – Charcoal Pencil Method

Transferring with Chalk

1. Neatly trace the pattern of the design onto tracing paper. You may use a pencil or a pen. It is not necessary to trace shading lines or curlicues.
2. Turn over the traced design. Firmly go over the traced lines on the back with chalk. (Photo 1) Do not scribble all over the tracing with the chalk.
3. Shake off the excess chalk dust, being careful not to inhale the particles.
4. Position the design on the prepared surface, chalk side down. Using a stylus, go over the lines. (Photo 2) Don't press so hard that you make indentations in the surface. The chalk will be transferred to your surface. Chalk is easily removed and it dissolves as you paint over it.

Photo 1 – Chalk Method

Photo 2 – Chalk Method

PAINTING SUPPLIES

About Acrylic Paints

There are marvelous acrylic paints for painting on all kinds of surfaces. It's important to choose the right paint for the surface. Cleanup is easy with soap and water.

On Wood, Fabric, Paper & Candles

You may use the patterns in this book to paint on surfaces such as wood, fabric, and paper surfaces. To paint, use **artist pigment acrylics**. These rich, creamy, opaque paints come in squeeze bottles and are available at art supply and craft stores. They have true pigment color names, just like oil paints. Their pigment is brilliant, and you can blend them and move them in much the same way as oil paints by using painting mediums.

Pre-mixed **acrylic paints** are available in hundreds of colors. These are not true pigment colors, but blended colors. They have the same consistency as artist pigment acrylics and can be used for decorative painting the same way as artist pigment acrylics.

On Glass & Ceramics

To paint on glass and ceramic surfaces, you'll want to use **acrylic enamels**, which are specially formulated to perform well on shiny and slick surfaces. These paints require no special preparation and are self-sealing and scratch-resistant. They can be air dried to cure or baked in a home oven for added durability.

On Outdoor Surfaces

To paint on surfaces you plan to use or display outdoors, such as metal watering cans, clay pots, and tiles, choose an **outdoor enamel** paint, which will hold up well in weather. When you use outdoor enamels, sealing isn't necessary.

On Paper

For painting on paper, you can use artist pigment acrylics and acrylic craft paints or choose an acrylic **paint for paper**. These paints are acid-free and can be used for dimensional, textured, or flat finishes. They are available in satin, metallic, and glitter sheens, but the range of colors is much more limited when compared with other acrylic paints.

Painting Mediums

Mediums are liquids or gels that are mixed with paint for achieving specific effects. They are sold along with acrylic paints. It's always best to use mediums and paints from the same manufacturer.

Mediums for Artist Pigment Acrylics

Floating medium is used to thin the paint so that it can be used for floating a color. The brush is filled with the floating medium, and a corner of the brush is then filled with color. After the brush is blended on the palette, the color is brushed along the edge of a design element to create a shading or highlighting.

Blending medium is used to keep paint wet and moving. The medium is brushed on the surface in the area of the design where you're going to paint, and the area is painted immediately while the blending medium is still wet.

Glazing medium is used to thin the paint so the mixture can be used as antiquing or to create transparent textured effects. The glazing medium is mixed with the paint on a palette or in a small container until a transparent consistency is reached. This medium can also be used as a substitute for floating medium. It works in the same way.

Textile medium is mixed with paint before the paint is applied to cloth. The paint will be permanent on the fabric when it dries.

Water can also be considered a medium. It thins paint for line work and washes.

Mediums for Acrylic Enamels

You don't want to use water to thin acrylic enamels. Always use the painting mediums specially manufactured for the paint you're using.

Clear medium works much like floating medium – it gives the paint a transparent quality.

Flow medium helps paint flow off the brush. It's helpful when painting line work or details.

Extender works like a blending medium. It gives the paint more open time, so you have more time to work the paint before it dries.

Mediums for Paper Paints

To use paper paints for brush work, you'll need to use a **flow medium** to thin the paint to the proper consistency.

HINTS FROM PRISCILLA

- Acrylic paints like to be cold. They won't dry as quickly if the room temperature is 68 degrees or colder. Heat dries, cold does not.

- Do not allow air to blow on your project while you're painting. Rapidly moving air dries the paint. Still air allows you more time to move the paint.

- Humidity keeps things wet. The higher the humidity, the more time you'll have for blending.

- Use a lot of paint so the colors will blend together.

My work area, ready for painting!

BRUSHES

There are many different types of brushes, and different-shaped brushes do different things. You will need four types of brushes in various sizes to do your decorative painting.

FLAT BRUSHES

Flat brushes are designed for brush strokes and blending. These brushes do most of the painting of the designs.

ROUND BRUSHES

Round brushes are used primarily for stroking – we seldom blend with them. They can also be used for some detail work.

FILBERT BRUSHES

Filbert brushes are a cross between a flat and a round brush. They are generally used for stroking, but can also be used for blending.

LINER BRUSHES

Liner brushes are very thin round brushes that come to a wonderful point. Good liner brushes are needed for fine line work.

When it comes to brushes, please purchase the very best that money can buy. They are your tools – the things you paint with. Occasionally, a student says, "Priscilla, I don't want to buy a good brush until I know I can paint." I always tell my students they won't be able to paint if they don't begin with a good brush. You get what you pay for.

Other Paint Applicators

- **Sponge brushes** can be used for basecoating and for applying varnish. They are usually 1" wide and inexpensive.

- **Stencil brushes** can be used to pounce or dab paint on surfaces.

- Round **sponge-on-a-stick applicators** are great for painting circular design motifs – you can find them in a variety of sizes. Smaller ones may be labeled "**daubers**."

BRUSH CARE

It's important to clean your brushes properly and keep them in excellent condition. To thoroughly clean them:

1. Gently flip-flop each brush back and forth in water until all the paint is removed, rinsing them thoroughly. Never slam brushes into a container and stir them.
2. Work brush cleaner through the hairs of the brush in a small dish and wipe the brush on a soft, absorbent rag. Continue cleaning until there is no trace of color on the rag.
3. Shape the brush with your fingers and store it so nothing can distort the shape of the hairs. Rinse the brush in water before using again.

Brush types, *pictured left to right*: Round, filbert, liner, flat.

BASIC SUPPLIES

In addition to paint, mediums, and brushes, these are basic painting supplies that
are needed for each painting project.

Tracing Paper - I like to use a very thin, transparent tracing paper for tracing designs. I use a **pencil** for tracing.

Brown Paper Bags - I use pieces of brown paper bags with no printing on them to smooth surfaces after basecoating and between coats of varnish.

Chalk, White and Colored - I use chalk for transferring the traced design to the prepared painting surface. Because chalk will easily wipe away and not show through the paint, I prefer it to graphite paper. Do not buy the dustless kind of chalk. I also use a **charcoal pencil** for transferring some designs.

Graphite Transfer Paper - Occasionally, I use white or gray graphite paper to transfer my design. However, I try to avoid using it because the lines may show through the paint. It can also make smudges on the background that are not easily removed.

Stylus - Use a stylus tool for transferring your traced design to the prepared surface. A pencil or a ballpoint pen that no longer writes also may be used.

Palette - I like to use a "stay-wet" type palette. Some people prefer a wax-coated or dry palette for acrylics; however, I prefer a palette that stays wet since acrylics dry so quickly. A wet palette consists of a plastic tray that holds a wet sponge and special paper. Palettes can be found where decorative painting supplies are sold.

Palette Knife - Use a palette knife for mixing and moving paint on your palette or mixing surface. I prefer a straight-blade palette knife made of flexible steel.

100% Cotton Rags - Use only 100% cotton rags for wiping your brush. *Try the knuckle test: For 15 seconds, rub your knuckles on the rag that you wipe your brush on. If your knuckles bleed, think of what that rag is doing to the hairs of your brush!* You could also use soft, absorbent **paper towels** for wiping brushes.

Water Basin: Use a water basin or other container filled with water for rinsing brushes.

Varnish: See "Finishing Your Piece" for details.

For projects on wood:

Sandpaper - I use sandpaper for smoothing unfinished and finished wood surfaces and for creating a distressed, aged look on painted surfaces. Sandpaper comes in various grades from very fine to very coarse. It's good to keep a supply on hand.

Tack Cloth - A tack rag or tack cloth is a piece of cheese-cloth or other soft cloth that has been treated with a mixture of varnish and linseed oil. It is very sticky. Use it for wiping a freshly sanded surface to remove all dust particles. When not in use, store the tack rag in a tightly sealed jar.

Wood Filler - Choose a good wood filler for filling holes, knots, and cracks. Follow the manufacturer's instructions for application.

Painting Techniques

Shading & Highlighting with Floating

Floating – flowing color on a surface – is a technique for adding shading and highlighting to design elements. Our example shows shading and highlighting floated on a leaf that has been undercoated in a gray-green (bayberry) color.

Photo 1. Before floating, undercoat the design element and let dry. Add a second or even a third coat, if necessary. Let dry.

Photo 2. Fill your brush with floating medium. (What size brush you use is determined by the size of the design.) *Option:* Use water in place of floating medium. Dip the brush in water and blot by gently pulling the brush along the edge of your water basin.

Photo 3. Fill one side of the brush with the shading color by stroking up against the edge of a puddle of paint.

Photo 4. On a matte surface, such as tracing paper or wet palette paper, blend, blend, blend on one side of the brush.

Photo 5. Then turn over the brush and blend, blend, blend on the other side, keeping the paint in the center. Be sure the brush is good and full of paint and that the color graduates through the brush from dark to medium to clear.

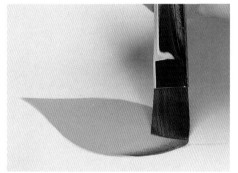

Photo 6. Float on the shading to the edge of the design element with the dark side of the brush towards the outside of the design. Let dry. Repeat the process, if desired, to deepen the color.

Photo 7. Float highlighting on the opposite side of the design, using the same technique as shading but with a light paint color.

Blending

For many designs, I do a very easy type of blending. A blending medium, which allows you to easily blend colors together, is used for this technique. First, neatly and carefully undercoat the design elements and let dry.

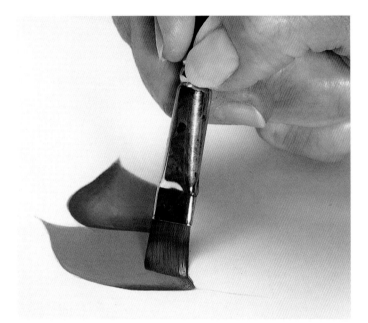

Photo 1. Float on the shadows. Let dry.

Photo 2. Add a small amount of blending medium to the area where you will be blending colors.

Photo 3. Add the colors you wish to blend on top of the wet blending medium.

Photo 4. Move the colors together to blend them, using an extremely light touch. NOTE: If you are heavy handed, you will wipe all the color away. If this happens, let the blending medium dry and cure and begin again *or* remove the color before it dries, add more blending medium, and begin again.

Flyspecking

Flyspecking adds an aged look to your pieces. To flyspeck, you need an old **toothbrush**, the **paint** color of your choice, **glazing medium**, a **palette knife**, and a mixing surface such as a **palette or plastic container**.

1. Place a small amount of the paint color on your mixing surface. Add glazing medium to the paint and mix with a palette knife to a very thin consistency. The thinner the paint, the finer the spatter. Thicker paint makes larger spatters.
2. Dip the toothbrush in the thinned paint. (Photo 1)
3. Hold the brush over the surface and pull your thumb across the bristles to spatter paint over the surface. (Photo 2) *Option:* Pull the palette knife across the bristles instead of your thumb.

Photo 1 – Loading a toothbrush with thinned paint.

Photo 2 – Flyspecking the surface.

PAINTING TIPS

• Avoid rinsing the brush too often in water. When loading a brush with a different color, but one that is in the same color family, it is preferable to wipe the brush on a damp paper towel to remove excess paint before loading a new color.

• When loading your brush with a color in a different color family, the brush does not need to be thoroughly cleaned. Simply rinse in water and blot brush on a paper towel to remove excess water. Then load the brush with a new color.

• Sometimes I paint with a "dirty brush." Leaving some of the color in the brush from another element seems to blend the colors together better. For example, if I want to add a reddish tint to a leaf, I will leave a little green in my brush when I load the red so that the colors can "marry."

Finishing Your Piece

Add a clear varnish or sealer to protect the painted surface. Choose a sealer or varnish that is compatible with the paint you used.

For some projects, a spray finish may be preferable. On wood surfaces, I apply two or more coats of brush-on **waterbase varnish** as follows:

1. Let the painting thoroughly dry and cure. Using a **synthetic bristle brush or sponge brush**, apply a coat of brush-on varnish. Let dry.
2. Rub the surface with a piece of a **brown paper bag** with no printing on it to smooth the surface.
3. Apply a final coat of varnish or a coat of clear **paste wax**.

Painting on Wood

Use acrylic paints or latex paints for basecoating and artist pigment acrylics
or acrylic paints for painting designs.

Preparing Old Wood

If the paint on an old piece is in good condition, cleaning the piece with soap and water and allowing it to dry completely may be all that's needed. To remove dirt, dust, cobwebs, or grease, use a cleaner that does not leave a gritty residue. Effective cleaners include **mild dishwashing detergent** and **bubble bath**. Mix the cleaner with water and wash with a cellulose sponge. Rinse and wipe dry with soft cloth rags. Let dry completely.

If the paint is chipped or flaking, but you want to keep the paint color and the old, distressed look, you will need to clean the piece and remove some of the chipped paint so your new painting won't flake away.

Here's how to prepare old paint:
1. Sand away any loose paint.
2. Wipe with a tack cloth.
3. Wipe with a liquid sanding preparation. Let dry thoroughly.
4. Transfer the design and proceed with painting.

Preparing New Wood

Generally, I don't seal raw wood before basecoating with acrylic paint because paint adheres better to unsealed wood. However, if there are knotholes or the wood is green, I apply a light coat of matte acrylic varnish to seal the flaws before applying paint.

Here's how to prepare new wood for painting:
1. Sand piece with medium, then fine grade sandpaper. Wipe with a tack cloth.
2. Apply a light coat of matte varnish to seal any knotholes or green wood. Let dry.
3. If the sealer has raised the grain of the wood, sand lightly with fine sandpaper and wipe with a tack cloth. Now you're ready to apply the basecoat. (See below.)

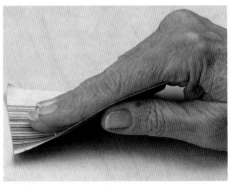
Sanding new wood.

Basecoating

The basecoat is the paint you apply to the surface before the design is transferred. If the paint on an old piece cannot be rescued or you don't like the color or if your piece is new, a fresh basecoat is necessary. Before you start, be sure the paint you apply is compatible with the type of paint you will use for the decorative painting. If you are not sure, take a sample of your paint to a good paint store and ask what type of paint you need.

Here's how to apply a new basecoat on an old piece:
1. Clean the surface.
2. Using medium grade sandpaper, sand the surface thoroughly.
3. Wipe with a tack cloth.
4. Apply a coat of stain-blocking primer or gesso. Allow to dry thoroughly and sand again. Wipe with a tack cloth.
5. Apply several coats of paint in your desired color, sanding between coats.

Here's how to basecoat a new piece:
1. With a small roller, a foam brush, or a synthetic bristle brush, apply a generous amount of paint. Let dry.
2. Rub with a piece of a brown paper bag with no printing on it to smooth the painted wood.
3. Apply a second coat of the base color if needed for complete coverage. Let dry.

Applying a basecoat to new wood with a foam brush.

4. Use a piece of a brown paper bag to smooth the surface again. Sometimes a third coat of paint is necessary for full coverage.

PAINTING ON GLASS & CERAMICS

Dishes, vases, bottles, jars, windows, canisters, lamps, tiles, teapots – the array of glass
and ceramic items to choose for painting is vast. Glass items can be clear, opaque, shiny, or
frosted, and they come in a variety of colors. Ceramic items can be glazed to create a
matte or glossy surface or unglazed (terra cotta pots, for example). Glass and ceramic
items can be plain or embossed.

Types of Paint

Use acrylic enamel paints on glass and ceramic surfaces –
they are self-sealing and scratch resistant. Some brands of
paint can be baked in a home oven for added durability.
Always follow the paint manufacturer's instructions for best
results. When cured or baked, painted glass and ceramic
items are waterproof and top-shelf dishwasher safe; however, do not allow a painted piece to soak in water.

You can use artist pigment acrylics or acrylic craft paints
on glass and ceramics, but the results are not as durable. For
ease of application and to improve adhesion, undercoat
designs with a glass and tile medium or spray with matte
sealer and allow to dry, then paint the design.

Preparing Glass & Ceramic Surfaces

Glass and ceramic surfaces don't require extensive preparation – basically, the surface should be clean and dry before
painting.

Here's how to prepare glass and ceramics:
• Wipe surface with rubbing alcohol and let dry.

• For sticky label residue or grease, use an adhesive remover.
• To remove surface dirt or dust, wash the item first with
soap and sudsy water, then wipe with rubbing alcohol on
a paper towel.

Using Patterns

There are options for using patterns on glass and ceramics, depending on the transparency or opacity of the piece.
• For simple designs, use the pattern as a guide and freehand the design.
• Trace the design on tracing paper. Position the pattern
and tape to the surface. If the surface is curved or irregular, it is helpful to cut away excess tracing paper. Slip a
sheet of transfer paper under the pattern and use a stylus
to transfer the design.
• If the item is clear or transparent glass, you can simply
place the pattern behind the glass (under a plate, inside a
vase, etc.) and tape it in place. You can see the pattern
through the glass. *Option:* Place the pattern behind the
glass and trace on the surface with a china marker,
crayon, or fine tip marker.

TIPS FOR WORKING WITH ACRYLIC ENAMELS

• Let the paint dry 30 minutes between coats.
• Work quickly because the paint dries quickly.
• Complete the painting within a 24-hour
period. (This helps ensure proper adhesion of
the layers.)
• When finished, let the piece air dry to cure
OR bake in your home oven, following the
manufacturer's instructions. Don't touch the
painted areas until the item has cooled
completely; the paint remains soft until it has
cooled.

Painting on Metal

There are many different types of metal surfaces we can paint on: some are slick and shiny, others are more porous. Since many metal items are meant to be used outdoors, how and where an item will be used also should be part of the decision of which paint to use and if a sealer is required.

Preparing Metal Surfaces

The preparation needed for metal items depends on the surface. Here are some guidelines:

- **Matte-finished surfaces:** If an item has been primed or painted with a matte finish paint, no preparation is required. Be sure the surface is clean and dry.
- **Galvanized tin items:** Remove the oily film by wiping with a sponge and a solution of three parts water, one part vinegar. Don't immerse the piece in water – water can become trapped and cause problems later. Allow to dry thoroughly before painting.
- **Painted, enameled, or slick surfaces:** Sponge with water and allow to dry.
- **Rusty surfaces:** Sand with sandpaper to remove rust. If rust is especially heavy, consider using a commercial rust-remover and follow the manufacturer's instructions. Let dry completely. Spray with metal primer or sealer, then paint.
- **Rusty-looking finishes:** Metal pieces with a sprayed-on "rusty" finish are easy to paint on – the paint creates a surface that's an interesting background for painted designs. Rust-inhibiting primers are often this red-brown, rusty color.

Types of Paint to Use on Metal

To paint on metal surfaces that are to be used indoors or outdoors, use **outdoor enamels** or weather-resistant **indoor/outdoor paint**. These paints are self-sealing and scratch-resistant. Additional sealers aren't required, and the paints are fade-resistant. Follow the manufacturer's guidelines regarding recommended painting mediums and whether or not the paint can be thinned with water.

You also can use **artist pigment acrylics and acrylic paints** on metal items. After the paint has dried and cured, apply several coats of varnish (choose an outdoor varnish for items to be used outdoors). I like to apply a coat of paste wax over the final coat of varnish.

Painting on Fabric

Clothing, tote bags, lamp shades, pillows, tablecloths, and napkins are just a few of the fabric surfaces than can be embellished with decorative painting.

Preparing Fabrics

If you wish to wash an item after you've painted it, you'll want to wash and dry the item according to the manufacturer's instructions before painting. Washing removes sizing and other fabric finishes that could interfere with paint adhesion. Press the fabric with an iron to smooth the surface and remove any wrinkles, then transfer the design with tailor's chalk or water-soluble transfer paper.

Types of Paint to Use

For permanent, washable painted designs on fabrics, use **textile medium** with **artist pigment acrylics or acrylic paints**. Choose a textile medium that's the same brand as your paint and follow the package instructions or this basic guideline: simply mix the paint colors with an equal amount of textile medium before beginning to paint.

Painting the Fabric

Cover a piece of heavy cardboard with plastic to create a firm, supportive surface for painting your fabric. Simply slip the covered board behind the fabric you're painting – it will protect other surfaces from paint that bleeds through the fabric. You can also use masking tape to hold the fabric taut as you paint.

You may find you need to load your brush more frequently when painting on fabric because the fabric absorbs the paint. After you have painted your design, allow 24 hours for the fabric to dry. Be sure to pull the fabric away from the plastic-covered cardboard so it doesn't stick to the board as it dries. Remove the board when the fabric is dry.

Heat Setting

Heat set your painted designs on items you plan to wash by pressing them with a dry iron. Place a pressing cloth over the design and hold the iron in place for 10 seconds, then move to another area. Continue until you've heat set the entire painted design. (You don't need to heat set items such as lamp shades, which won't be washed.)

Do you need to iron on the wrong side of the fabric? No – acrylic paints are flat on the surface and absorbed by the fabric, so nothing is raised or sticky.

Option: Place large items in a clothes dryer for 10 minutes to heat set.

BEAUTIFUL FLOWER PATTERNS

Flowers are so beautiful and delicate – they are one
of God's great gifts to us. I love painting all kinds of flowers
and have included patterns for daisies and daffodils,
roses in all their glory, cornflowers and chrysanthemums,
sturdy tulips, and the delicate blossoms of violets,
pansies, and forget-me-nots. I hope you enjoy painting
these lovely gifts from nature.

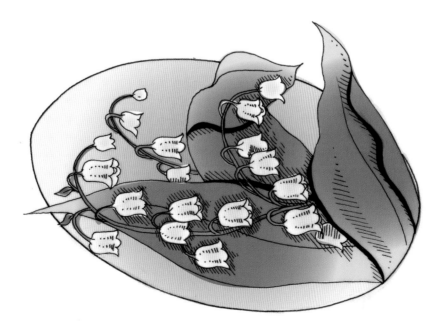

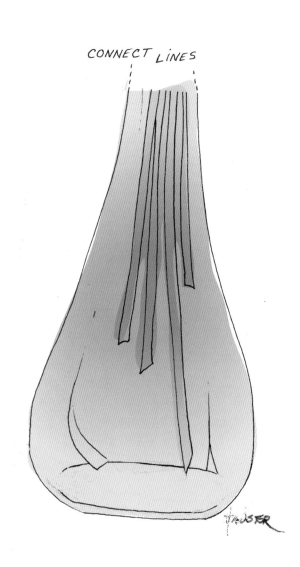

CONNECT LINES

TAUSER

36

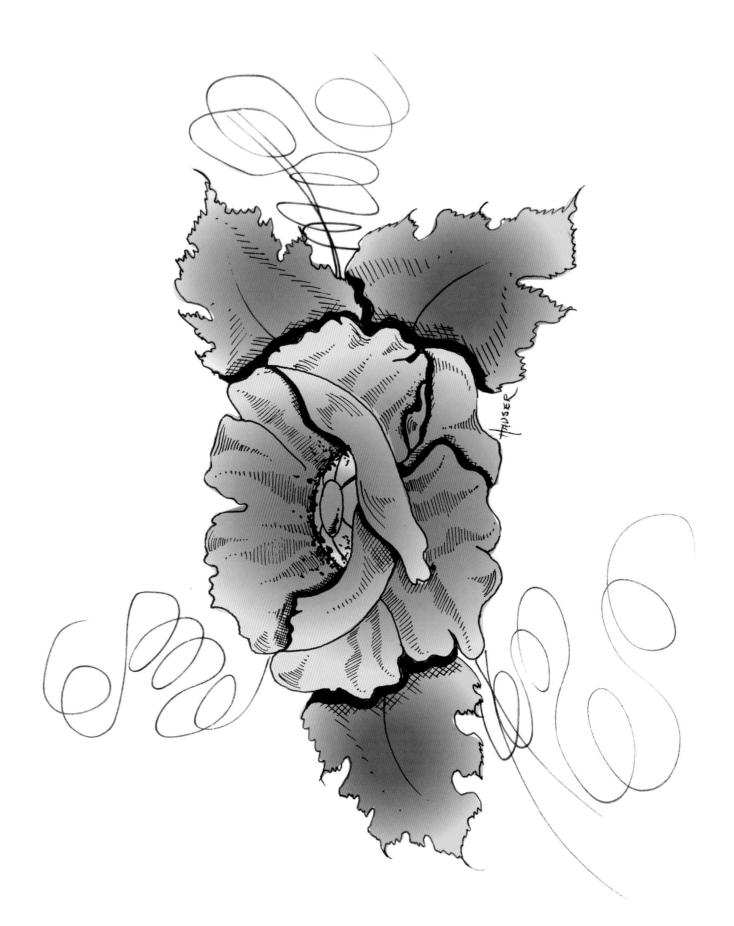

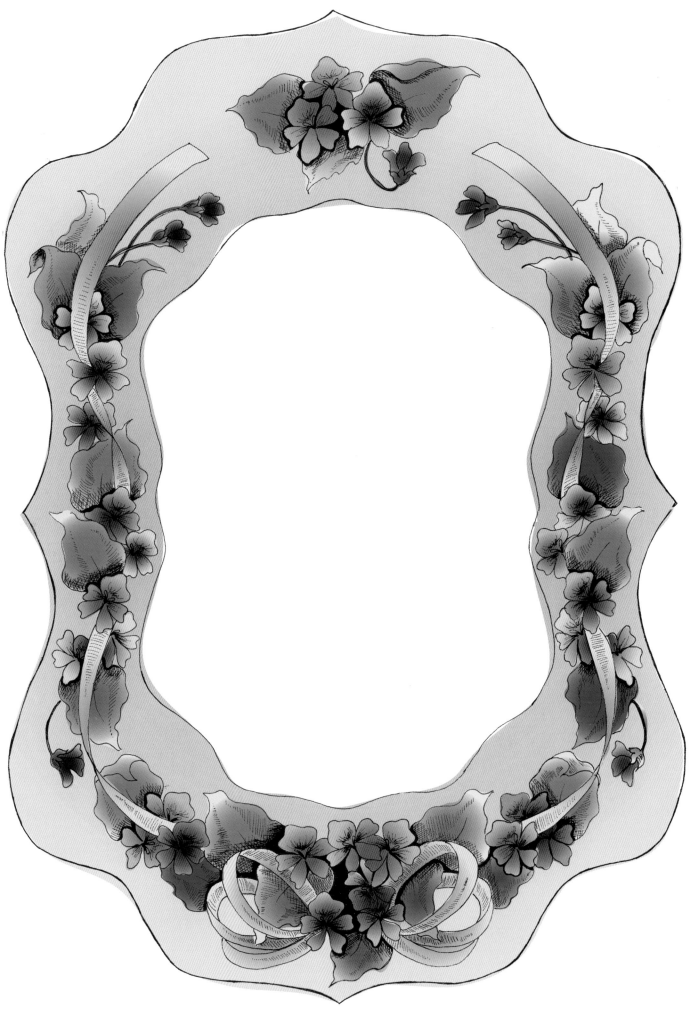

48

51

55

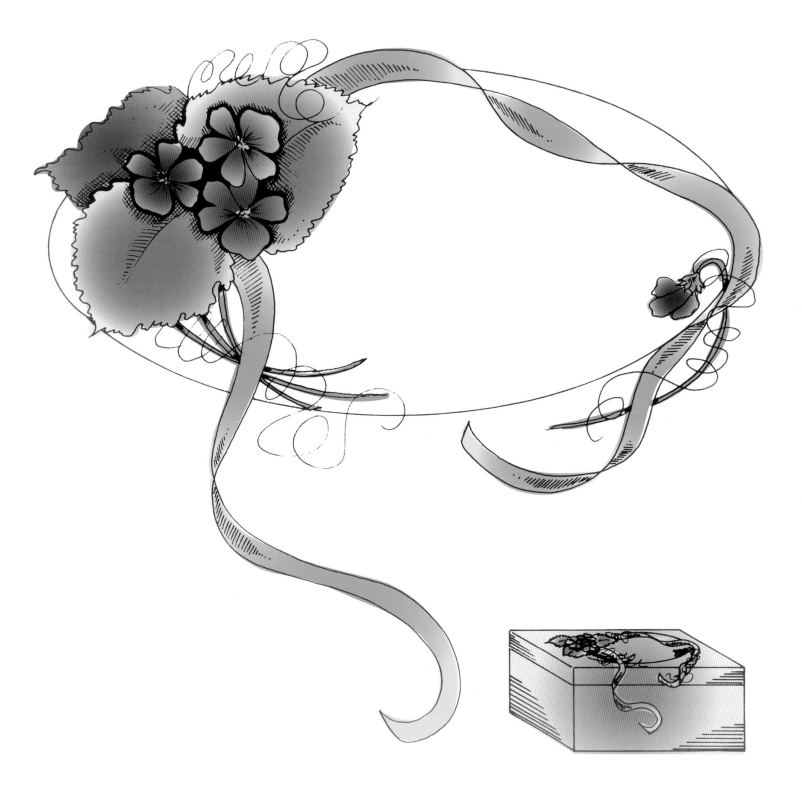

Happy
Pansy Faces
Lifted
to
The Sun

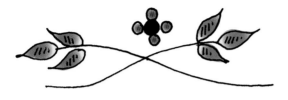

FRUIT & VEGETABLE PATTERNS

Painting fruits and vegetables is another way to celebrate the harvest, capture summer's bounty, and rejoice in nature's colorful beauty. You'll find patterns for a variety of fruits and vegetables, in containers, on the vine, and on their own. These patterns are wonderful painted on item for the kitchen – even on furniture.

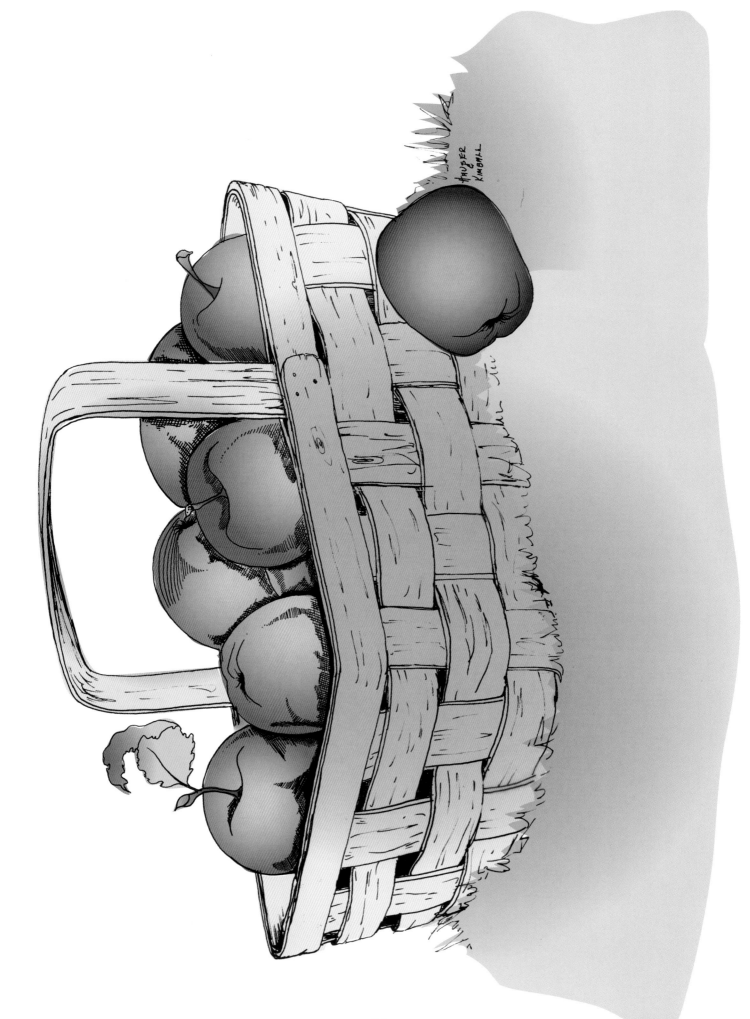

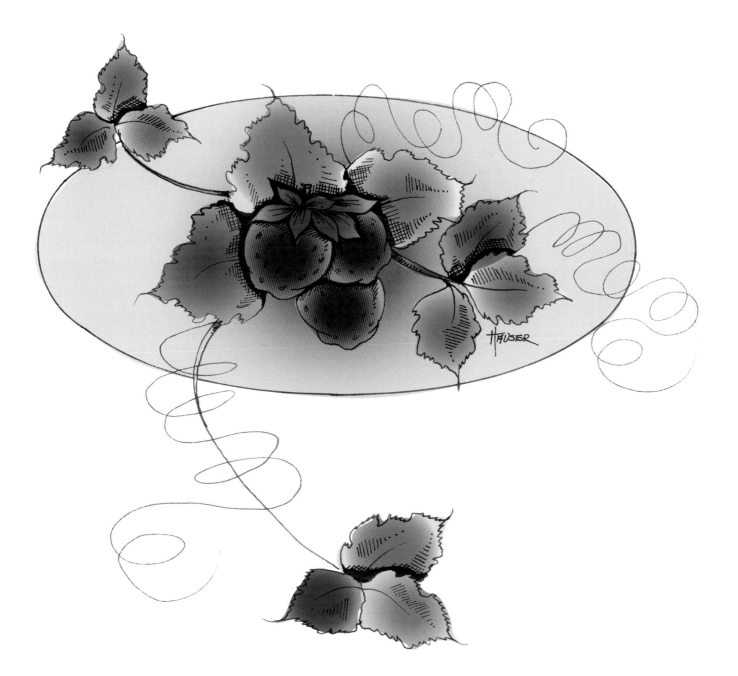

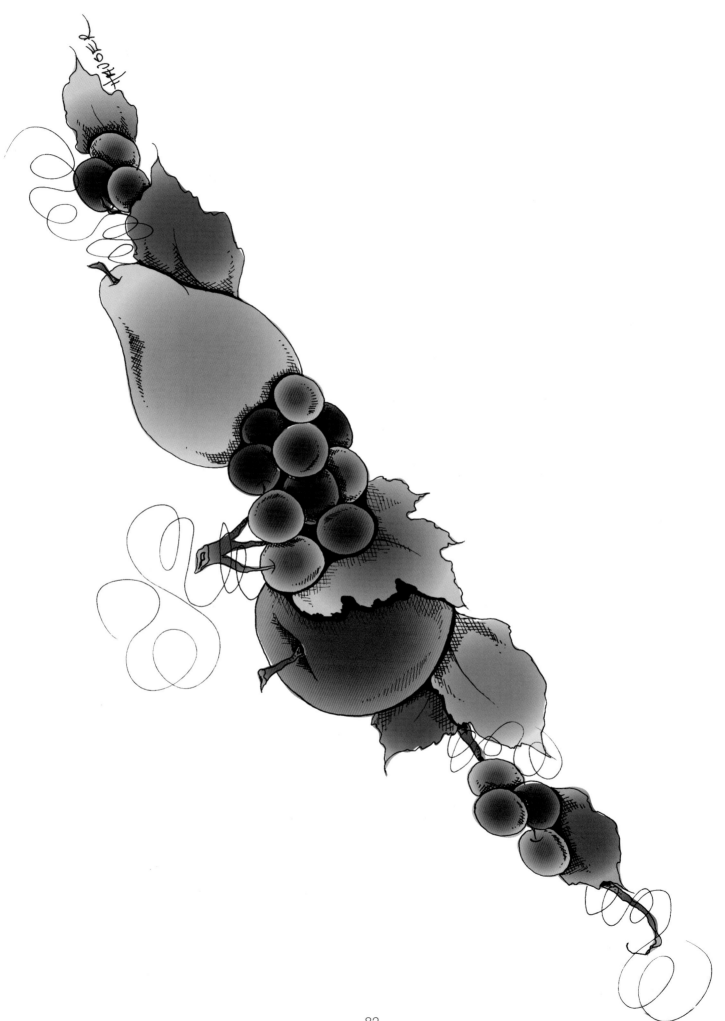

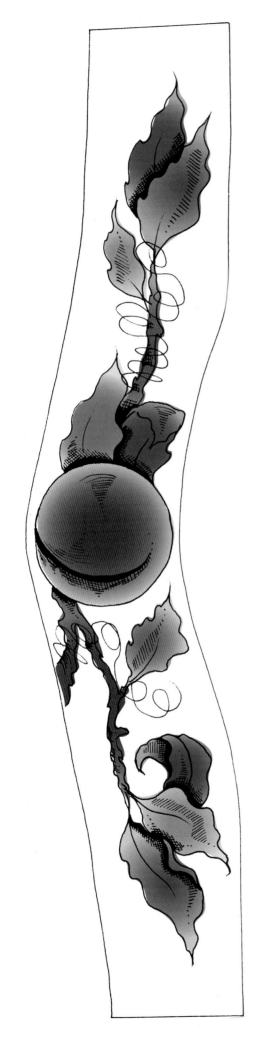
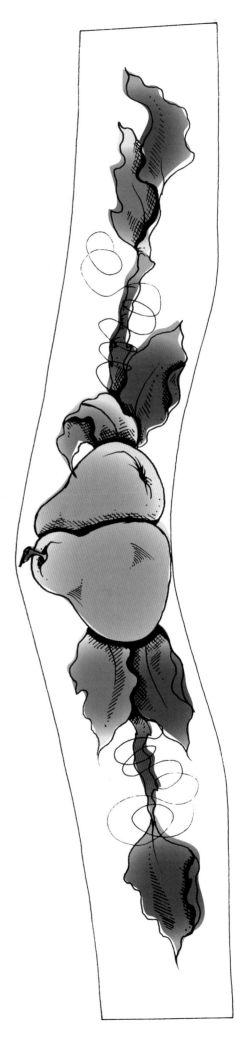

90

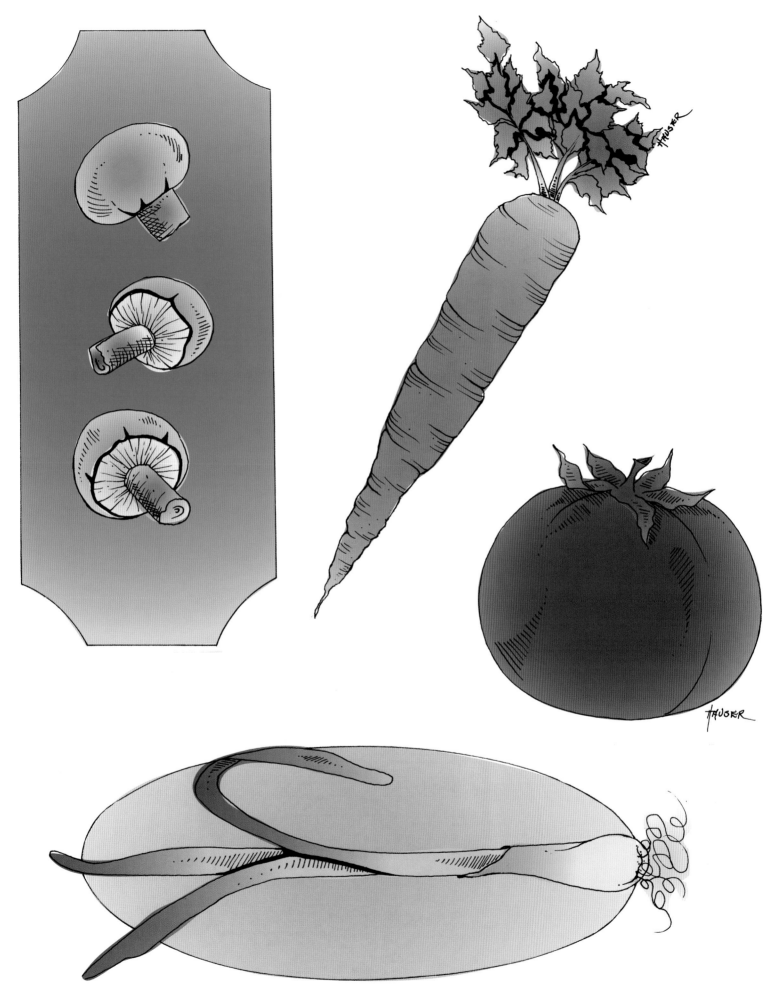

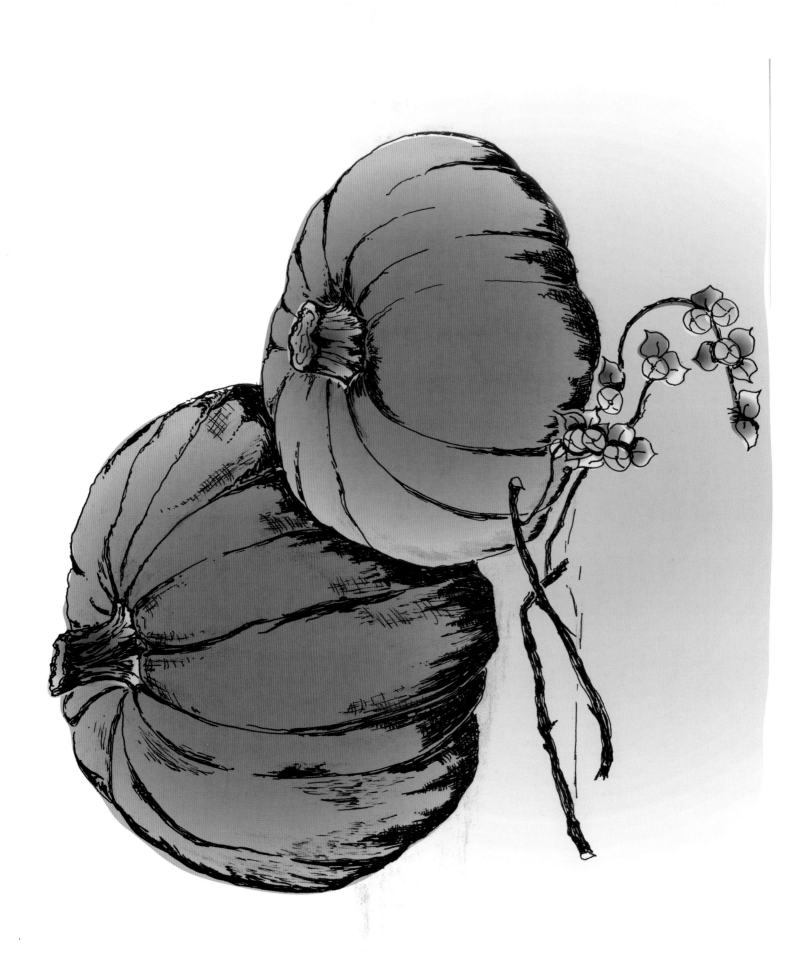

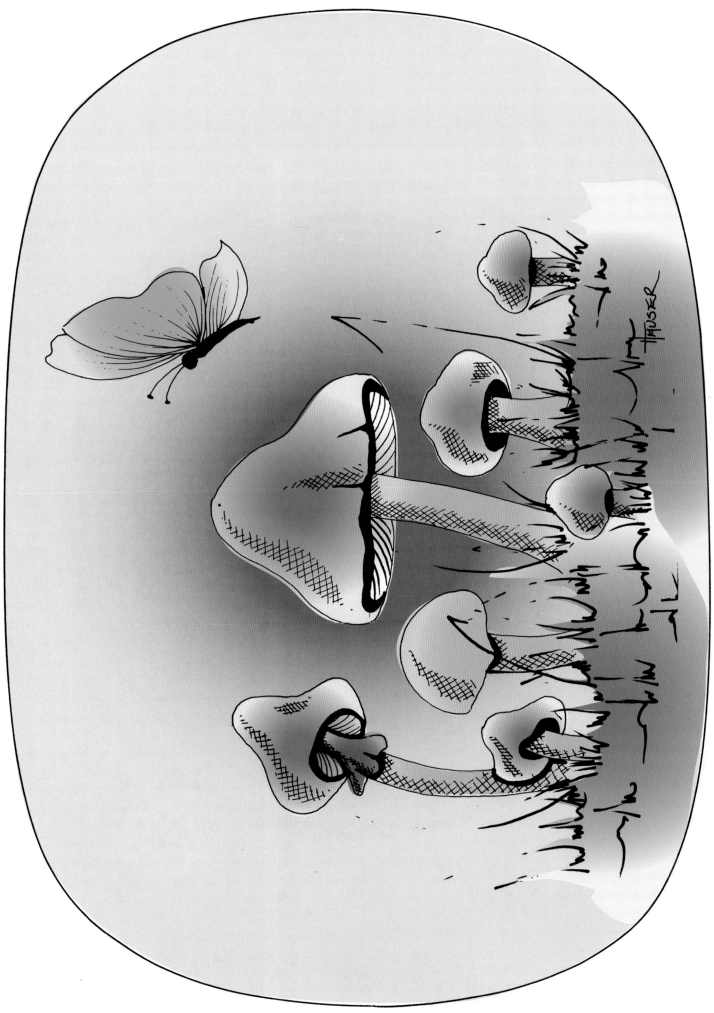

ANIMALS
BIRDS
BEES
&
THE SEAS

What's your favorite animal? A fish? A bird? A bee?
A butterfly? You'll find patterns for all of those and
more in this section.

A
LITTLE
SOMETHING
EXTRA

This section includes patterns for folk art inspired
strokes and borders, leaves, bottles, and seashells
among others. Use them individually as
focal points or borders or combine them
with other patterns.

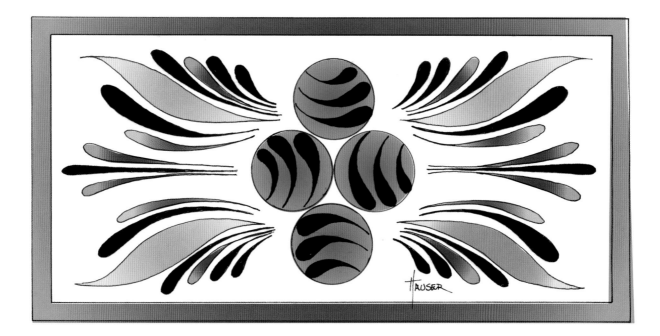

HOLIDAY
PATTERNS

Use these motifs to decorate boxes and banners and
to create wonderful holiday ornaments for your tree
or to give as gifts. Use them to celebrate the season.

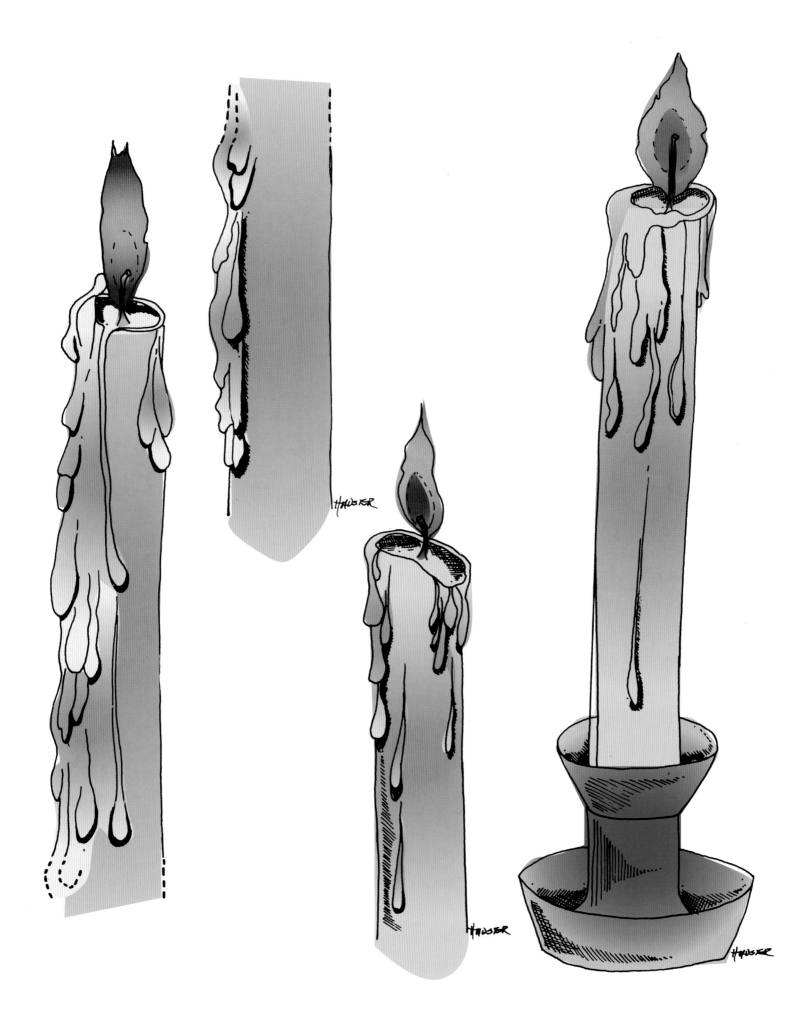

METRIC CONVERSION CHART

Inches to Millimeters and Centimeters

Inches	MM	CM	Inches	MM	CM
1/8	3	.3	2	51	5.1
1/4	6	.6	3	76	7.6
3/8	10	1.0	4	102	10.2
1/2	13	1.3	5	127	12.7
5/8	16	1.6	6	152	15.2
3/4	19	1.9	7	178	17.8
7/8	22	2.2	8	203	20.3
1	25	2.5	9	229	22.9
1-1/4	32	3.2	10	254	25.4
1-1/2	38	3.8	11	279	27.9
1-3/4	44	4.4	12	305	30.5

Yards to Meters

Yards	Meters	Yards	Meters
1/8	.11	3	2.74
1/4	.23	4	3.66
3/8	.34	5	4.57
1/2	.46	6	5.49
5/8	.57	7	6.40
3/4	.69	8	7.32
7/8	.80	9	8.23
1	.91	10	9.14
2	1.83		

About the Artist

She's the "First Lady of Decorative Painting," and with good reason. Due to Priscilla's efforts, dreams, and ability to draw people to her, the first meeting of the National Society of Tole & Decorative Painters took place on October 22, 1972 with 21 other people attending. Since then the organization has thrived, and so has Priscilla.

From Priscilla's beginning efforts as a tole painter in the early 1960s, having taken tole painting classes at a YMCA in Raytown, MO, she has become a world renowned teacher, author, and the decorative painting industry's ambassador to the world. She has used nearly every outlet to share her enthusiasm for and knowledge of decorative painting. Besides teaching all over the world, Priscilla has illustrated her technique through books, magazine articles, videos, and television. The results of her teaching method have lead to an accreditation program for teachers. She has traveled to teach in Canada, Japan, Argentina, and The Netherlands, as well as extensive teaching within the United States at her "Studio by the Sea" in Panama City Beach, Florida.

For information about Priscilla Hauser Painting Seminars,
you can contact Priscilla as follows:
Priscilla Hauser
P.O. Box 521013, Tulsa, OK 74152
Fax: (918) 743-5075
Phone: (918) 743-6072
Website: www.priscillahuaser.com
email: phauser376@aol.com

INDEX